It doesn't matter what kind of body you have. What matters is what you do with your life, and how you do it.

I've had a fat body my whole life. I can't remember what it's like not to be fat.

My body is ill and it often hurts, so sometimes I drop things and that bugs me.

After my operation I had a big scar on my body. At first I tried to hide it. But I've decided to accept my body as it is.

My eyes are beautiful. When I open them wide, they look like sparkling crystal plates.

I'm not that tall, but I actually think that's cool. I can fit under places where other people bump their heads.

I'm pretty happy with the way I look when I'm dressed but not when I'm naked.

I have a very hairy body. I like it a lot.

Sometimes I like my body, because I remember that this is what carries me through life. My feet carry me to beautiful places, my belly holds my organs, and my butt gives me a comfortable cushion to sit on. My arms allow me to hug the people I love.

I'm the smallest person in my class. I hope I'll grow soon.

It's kind of cool having a body, but it's not really that big a deal. Being smart is what's cool!

Sometimes I get annoyed at my body when it gives me pain or pimples. But I annoy it, too, when I eat unhealthy food or don't get enough exercise.

A body is funny because it's kind of just my shell. What would I be without my body? What would I be then?

I only have to please myself. And if you don't accept me the way I am, too bad for you!

AnyBody

A Comic Compendium of
Important Facts & Feelings about Our Bodies

Katharina von der Gathen ★ Anke Kuhl

AnyBody

A Comic Compendium of
Important Facts & Feelings about Our Bodies

Translated by Shelley Tanaka

GECKO PRESS

What's in this book?

Hello!

Everyone in the world has a body that they live with and can feel at home in. You wouldn't be you without your body. Most of the time it works without you even thinking about it. Sometimes it does what it wants. Maybe sometimes you wish your body would behave differently. But what a great feeling you get when you accomplish something fabulous with your body!

This book helps you think about how bodies work—your body and other people's bodies. You can read this book with your friends and find out how you're different and what you have in common. You can ask your parents and relatives questions and laugh at things you find strange or funny. Or you can just find out on your own what your one-of-a-kind body can do.

We have written and illustrated a number of books together that are based on the questions children have asked in classes and workshops on sex education and puberty. This book too began with questions and answers, from a survey we conducted in 2020, in which we asked wide-ranging questions about how people see their bodies and how they feel others see them. We received over 2500 responses. We were very moved by everyone's honest answers, which helped us shape this book and appear throughout the text and illustrations.

Katharina von der Gathen & Anke Kuhl

One of a kind

Each person is unique. No one else has ever been exactly like you, and there will never be anyone exactly like you again. From the moment an egg and sperm join, a lot about a person is already decided. You may inherit some things from your mother, others from your father. Certain gestures or body features may be similar to those of ancestors who died long ago. New babies are made up of a special mix of physical and personality traits—new and old, outer characteristics and inner ones.

Hair

HAIR EVERYWHERE

We have hair all over our bodies. The only places hair doesn't grow is on our lips, the palms of our hands and the soles of our feet.

Hair has always provided good protection for humans. Millions of years ago, our ancestors had fur all over their bodies, and the hair that remains on human bodies today serves an important function. The hair on our head protects us from the hot sun. Eyebrows help prevent sweat from dripping into our eyes. Armpit hair can help sweat evaporate. And when you stroke someone's skin, tiny hairs transmit that feeling over and beneath their skin.

If our ancestors could see us now...

HEAD HAIR

Hair comes in many different shades and textures. Everyone has their own mix of the two basic shades— black-brown and yellow-red. Most people are dark-haired. Relatively few are blond, and redheads are the rarest of all. As you get older, your hair gradually turns gray or white because the body no longer produces as much pigment. Hair grows out of our heads kinky, curly, wavy or straight.

NEW HAIR

When you first notice hair around your vulva or penis or under your armpits, you know that puberty is beginning. There may also be new and denser hair on your legs and arms, on parts of your butt, or on your upper lip, chin, chest, shoulders and back. Some young people can't wait for these signs that they are developing into an adult; for others the changes come too soon.

If you're wondering how hairy you might become when you're older, take a look at adults in your family. New hair grows gradually, so you'll have time to get used to it.

Skin

The skin is the body's biggest organ. As the body's outer covering, it protects the body and helps keep it warm or cool. Our skin allows us to make contact with other people through touch. Every person's skin also has its own distinct smell. Human skin has to withstand a lot every day. It is cleaned, creamed, wiped, painted, soaped, shaved, covered, soaked, injured, scratched, stroked, chilled, squeezed, rubbed, stretched, pressed, scrubbed, warmed and clothed.

MELANIN

Everyone has their own unique skin tone—a combination inherited from their parents. The more pigment, or melanin, in the skin, the darker it is. Melanin protects the skin from the sun's radiation. When your skin gets darker from being exposed to the sun, it's trying to protect itself. People with darker complexions are naturally better protected. But everyone's skin needs protection from the sun—people of all skin tones should use sunscreen.

Skin reactions

red   pale   blotchy

Skin features

Left to right, from top row: moles, freckles, birthmark, wart, stretch marks, varicose veins, goosebumps, scar from a caesarean section, pimples, rash, uneven melanin, tattoos.

MOLES & BIRTHMARKS

Almost everyone has little dark spots on their bodies. These occur when there's a lot of pigment in one place. Many babies are born with birthmarks, usually harmless marks or growths, which can be permanent or fade over time. Others have freckles or moles. Freckles are smooth spots that appear in clusters, while moles are often raised single spots. Many people get age spots or liver spots as they age.

All of these skin spots—sometimes known as beauty marks—can change over time, depending on each person's predisposition and how much their skin is exposed to sunshine. Moles and skin marks that change or itch can be a sign of a skin problem, so need to be checked by a doctor.

STRETCH MARKS

Stretch marks look like fine, shimmery streaks on the skin where the underlying tissue has been slightly torn. They're most common on the belly, inner thighs or breasts. Stretch marks don't hurt, and anyone can have them—children who grow quickly, adolescents developing their adult bodies, pregnant people, and people who have developed muscles through exercise or gained or lost weight in a short period of time.

SCARS

Skin can be scarred if it has been deeply injured from cuts, burns, disease or an accident. Behind every scar lies a story of pain or even adventure. For people whose children have been born by caesarean section, a short scar below the belly button remains as a reminder. After a difficult operation, many people consider their scars a mark of survival— I made it!

PIMPLES

Almost all young people have problems with pimples. Most of the time these are caused by hormones that come with puberty. But adults get pimples, too, from time to time. They might be caused by stress, bacteria, too much sun, diet or heredity. If you have a lot of stubborn pimples, it is called acne. You can help by keeping skin clean and eating healthy food, and maybe seeing a doctor or dermatologist. Sometimes it's just a matter of waiting, so the skin can help itself. We tend to worry more about our pimples than the people around us do.

WARTS

Warts are small bumps that usually appear on your fingers, between your toes or on the soles of your feet. Many children have them at some stage. Even though they usually don't hurt, warts are annoying, and they can spread. You can treat them with a caustic liquid or by freezing them. If you wait long enough, warts will often disappear by themselves. Wishing them away can work too—just kidding!

Getting naked

All humans are born naked. You're naked when you get dressed and undressed or when you're in the shower or bath. Most people are also naked when they have sex. But not everyone likes to look at their naked body in the mirror, and each person feels differently about nudity at different times and stages of life. It's different for every family, too.

Some people are very comfortable with naked bodies because it's part of their job. Many caregivers, photographers, massage therapists, artists or tattoo artists are used to working with people when they're not fully dressed. Actors may appear stark naked on a stage or film set. Doctors and nurses are also used to seeing people naked, but for some patients it can take a major effort to undress for an examination.

Did you know?
In Ancient Greece, nudity was completely normal in many daily activities. Men would be naked when participating in sports and combat lessons.

It is always your choice whether to be naked or not.

Everyone is naked beneath their clothes!

Body fluids

Fluids and solids flow, drip and ooze from openings in our bodies. The things that come out of us can be slimy or thick, watery or dry. The body produces them for many reasons, including to carry waste materials out of the body, to ward off bacteria, to keep parts of the body moist, and to make food for babies.

Breasts only produce **breast milk** when nursing a baby. Breast milk tastes a bit different each day, depending on what the mother has been eating.

Menstrual blood is actually a mixture of mucous membrane, fluids and blood.

Cervical mucus is a white discharge caused by hormones. It changes throughout the menstrual cycle.

Smegma is a pale, slightly crumbly substance that has a cheesy smell. You might find it now and then between the glans and foreskin of your penis or between the skin folds of your vulva.

During ejaculation, a gush of **semen** comes out of the penis. Some people say it smells like chestnut blossoms. Others think it smells like bleach.

It can sometimes be a good thing to be a bit turned off by certain things that come out of our bodies because these substances can also carry bacteria and disease.

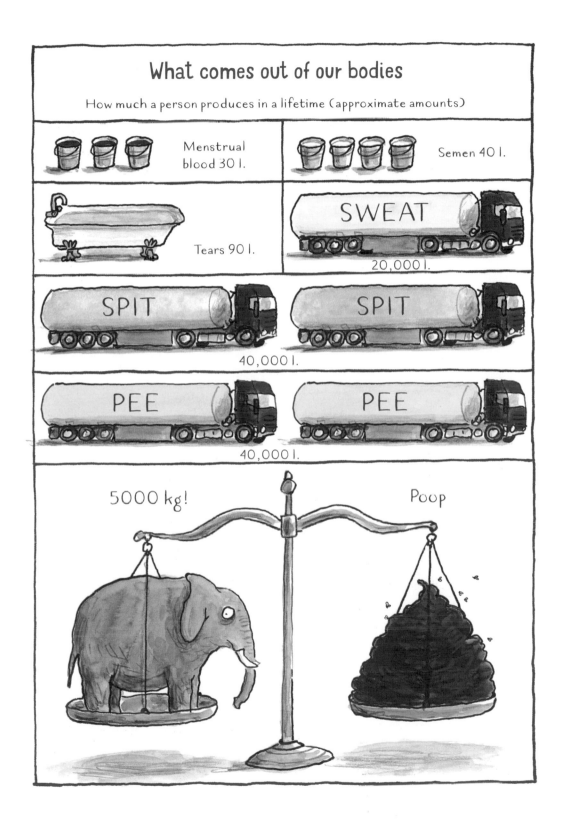

Body quirks

Can your body do any of these things?
Some of these are quirks you can inherit; others can be learned with practice.

Breasts

Both boys and girls have breasts. You start to see a difference when puberty begins (often around the age of ten to twelve but sometimes earlier or later). You can never know ahead of time how big your breasts will be and what shape they will take. But you can get a sense of how they might look by looking at your mother, grandmother or sister.

Breasts contain nerves, fatty tissue and mammary glands that branch out in small passages, or ducts, through the breasts to the nipple. The mammary glands are small and unnoticeable until they're needed to produce milk to nourish a baby.

Mammary glands
in the breasts

Breasts don't feel the same every day. Some days they may feel fairly soft. On other days they may feel firm and plump. Some days they may feel slightly bigger, depending on which hormones are active in the body.

Boys can also develop thicker and more sensitive breasts during puberty. They will go back to their earlier shape once puberty is over.

Vulva & vagina

Some people say vagina and others say vulva, depending on which term they learned at home or school. It's good to know the difference between the two. Strictly speaking, you can only see the entrance to the vagina, which is a kind of inside passage, about the length of a finger, that leads from the outside to the uterus. Everything else that you see on the outside belongs to the vulva. If you have a vulva, you can use a mirror to see the soft outer labia or lips with two smaller inner lips. If you gently pull these aside, you can see the opening that is the vagina and, above this, the small opening that is the urethra. The urethra connects to the bladder, so this is the hole where pee comes out. At the front there is a kind of hood with a little knob. This is the visible part of the clitoris, which is very sensitive to touch. Every vulva looks different—there are almost four billion versions around the world.

Did you know?
The clitoris is an important organ that provides pleasure for girls and women. Yet for centuries it was excluded from scientific anatomy illustrations.

Intersex

Sometimes when a baby is born, you can't tell for sure if it is male or female. The baby's body may have developed both male and female characteristics, such as a penis on the outside and ovaries on the inside. Sometimes it isn't clear whether a baby has a very small penis or a long clitoris, because they look similar. This child is intersex, which means they have both male and female sexual parts. Some intersex people identify as a boy or a girl, some identify as neither or both.

Penis

Penises are for peeing, to feel pleasure, or to help make a baby. The tip of the penis, which is very sensitive, is called the glans. At birth this is hidden under a retractable foreskin, but it is exposed in people who have been circumcised. Circumcision is when the foreskin is removed a few weeks after birth. It is fairly common in different cultures for religious and health reasons.

Did you know?
Hardly any penises are straight like a ruler. Especially when they are stiff, you can see that most penises bend a bit to the left or to the right.

In the scrotum, which is found behind the penis, are two little balls called testicles. This is where sperm cells are produced.

During sex or masturbation, semen containing sperm can come out of the tip of the penis and provide a great feeling of pleasure. The penis and scrotum can be soft and relaxed or firm and hard, or anywhere in between.

Every penis is different and one of almost four billion versions in the world. None of them look the same.

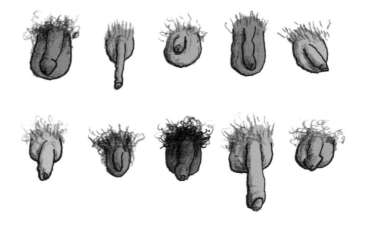

25

Body size

Most people go through periods of being a little thinner or a little fatter at different times in their lives, depending on the circumstances. There can be any number of reasons why someone is particularly fat or thin, and when you first meet them, you may have no idea what those reasons are. Sometimes they know the reason for their body size and sometimes they don't. Either way, it can be annoying and frustrating when other people focus on their body size.

Many people think you need to be thin to be beautiful. Advertising and social media mostly show people who are slim and athletic also looking happy and content. But this isn't reality. Some people would love to be slimmer, while others would love to be a bit heavier or more muscular, or to have a fuller figure. Often your body shape is inherited from your parents; there's usually not much you can do to change it.

Everyone has their own idea of how they should look to feel at their best, even though others would barely notice the difference. It's best to pay attention to what feels right for your own body. What other people have to say about it doesn't really matter.

There are degrees of thinness and fatness that can be harmful for different people and at different ages. Relatives, therapists and doctors can help with the thoughts, feelings and behaviors that affect body size.

Family reunion 1998

Bernard

Mary

Giselle

John

Helena

Tina

Louis

28

See how we look later, on pages 34, 48 and 68.

Pain

It can really hurt when you fall down during a game of tag, or when you're lying in bed with an ear infection or bad stomach cramps. Pain is an important warning signal. Your body is saying, "Pay attention, I'm in danger." It needs care and rest. For someone in pain, nothing else exists in that moment. Nothing else matters. Having someone there to comfort and support you is particularly important.

Physical illness

When you have a fever or a bad cold, your body can feel completely worn out for a while. You just want to lie in bed, be looked after and not have to do anything important. Sometimes people may also have a serious illness that's not going away any time soon. Their body may need lots of care and sometimes strong medications. They may need others to look after them and stay with them. To pass the time, you can watch movies together, tell jokes, make plans, and keep your fingers crossed that things will soon get better. Some illnesses are chronic, which means people have to live with them for many years, or a lifetime. When this happens, we are reminded how society is set up for people with healthy bodies.

Mental illness

The body isn't the only thing that can get sick. A person's mind can become ill, too, and this isn't always easy to spot from the outside. Depression is a particularly common mental illness. People suffering from depression feel unwell over a long period of time. They barely have the strength to do everyday things like schoolwork or shopping. Some people don't want to talk to anyone anymore, or they can't sleep properly at night. They feel like their lives will be dark forever. Both children and adults who suffer from depression need help from professionals who know about the condition and can help them get well again. Friends and family are also very important.

Disability

Some people have a disability that can prevent them from moving or perceiving things in a way that they might want to. You could say these people have different abilities and that the world is set up to be easy for some people and difficult for others. For example, having only stairs and no ramp into a building or vehicle will mean some people can't get access. If children in school are given tasks that are too difficult for them, they won't learn properly. If no one translates into sign language, it could prevent people who can't hear well from being able to understand. Many of these situations can be improved just by being aware of the range of abilities among people.

Did you know?
Very few people are born with a disability. Most disabilities come about as a result of illness or an accident.

Disabilities can affect our bodies and minds. They can affect a person's sight, movement, thinking, learning, hearing, mental health or social relationships. "Disabled people" are not a single group but a whole range of people with different needs.

For a disabled person, and for their families and friends, their disability is pretty normal. It is part of who they are. Newcomers may not be sure how best to behave. As you spend more time together, you'll learn from each other and quickly figure it out.

When you talk about somone's disability, it's always good to listen to how they talk about themselves—or you could ask directly what words they prefer you to use.

Clear the way!

Family reunion 2006

Henry
Hilda
Vera
Mary
Frida

Herbie
Ella

See page 28 for how we used to look.

Louis

Helena

Tina

John

Giselle

See pages 48 and 68 for what we look like later on.

Body & soul

A person is more than a physical body that you can see and touch. We are also made up of thoughts, feelings, ideas, dreams and personalities. Outside and inside, the body and soul are tightly bound together. What you think and feel on the inside can directly affect your body. If you are particularly happy or in love, your heart may beat faster. Hormones can also affect your mood. It can also work the other way: your body can affect what you feel on the inside. You feel joy and pride after climbing a mountain or doing something else challenging.

Beauty ideals

For thousands of years, people have thought about what makes a person beautiful. Scientists have discovered that people are considered to be particularly attractive when both sides of the body are as symmetrical as possible—with eyes of the same size and the same distance from the nose, say, or even shoulders. But of course no one's face or body is actually symmetrical!

Ideals of beauty change, just like fashions change. You can see this if you look at photographs of models and actors from the past.

People's perceptions of what is beautiful are different everywhere in the world and among different groups. Racism and colonialism have influenced ideas about ideal beauty, often in harmful ways.

Even when you have a pretty good idea of what is considered beautiful in general, each person still has specific ideas of how they want to look—even when that may be impossible for their particular body type.

Feeling attractive (or not)

Try this!
Take the opportunity to observe other people—on the bus, in the schoolyard, in a waiting room. It's like hunting for treasure! What is it about them that you find special or beautiful? Sometimes you'll only notice these things when you take the time to look. "Looking for treasure" can be a fun thing to do with your friends, too. Afterwards you can share what you noticed with each other.

It can be great fun to celebrate the beauty of your own body, to wear cool clothes or get dressed up to go out. And if you think that others also notice how good you look, that can feel good too!

It feels pretty horrible to look at yourself and think you're ugly. As soon as you look in the mirror, you see only one thing—maybe a large nose, or skinny legs, or pimples on your face. But no particular feature is objectively more or less beautiful than another one. You are nowhere near as critical when you look at other people, when it's easier to notice their great personality or laugh more than individual body parts.

40

Looking good also depends on which community and culture you belong to. And sometimes what others like best about you is the very thing that you find ugly about yourself. Each person can feel better or worse about their own body depending on the day; even if you look the same on the outside, it can feel very different to you.

Look at this horrible long neck...

It's gorgeous!

Try this!

Ask your friends or family members to write down what they find beautiful about you and what they like about you. Collect these notes in a nice box or jar. On days when you are unsure about your looks, read a few of those notes. Everything you read is an honest comment, and it is true!

It can feel really good to look at your own body with pleasure and feel comfortable with it. Other people may admire you for feeling this way, or they may envy you. There's nothing wrong with taking some time to admire yourself. When you've had enough of that, you can go out and discover all the other beautiful people and things around you.

41

Gender

Gender is the way we feel inside about who we are, while sex has more to do with body parts and biology. When a baby is born, most people assume they know the baby's gender based on the appearance of their body and whether they have male or female genitals. We now understand that gender is more than just two opposites; it is a whole range of feelings and ways of being.

Try this

You might not know a person's gender identity when you first meet them. Try using the pronoun "they," which refers to any gender—it's nice not to make assumptions.

There are many ways to be male, female, masculine, feminine, trans, non-binary, genderqueer, boy, girl, and many other words people use to describe themselves. Sometimes this is called the "gender spectrum," to show that gender is a scale with many stops along the way.

GENDER SPECTRUM

Some people feel more in the middle of the gender spectrum. They may identify as non-binary, agender or genderqueer. Some might feel comfortable with their assigned gender but want to express themselves differently to others of the same gender. Others come to know during puberty or as adults that their feelings about their gender don't match what others assume about them.

Trans

A trans person might feel that the body they are born with doesn't match who they are. A person born with a vagina who identifies as a boy is a trans boy, and a person born with a penis who identifies as a girl is a trans girl. It can be challenging and complicated for trans kids and their families. It can take years to figure everything out. At some point they might feel comfortable enough to tell classmates, friends and teachers. For the child it's an important step. Now they can finally be seen the way they have always felt inside. Sometimes trans people change their names, their appearance, their bodies—it's up to each person to decide how they want to present themselves.

Girls & boys

Some people say it's pretty simple. Girls have a vagina. They like red and pink. They love horses and glitter, to read, draw and wear makeup. Boys have a penis, they like blue and they like to run around outdoors or play computer games. Boys like to show off their muscles, they watch action films and love wild adventures.

It's not like that. Each girl and boy is their own person. You can be sassy and anxious, a karate master and gardener; you can play in a band, love dancing and have a huge dinosaur collection. You can be shy and loud, like both unicorns and martial arts, be a loving parent to your dolls or bake a cake for your best friend while wearing a superhero costume. Every person has many different sides to them.

Scientists have long discussed gender differences. How much are we born with certain preferences and traits? How much are we influenced by the people around us?

Did you know?
Until the mid 20th century, little girls were often dressed in light blue. Blue represented the purity and innocence of the Virgin Mary, who in many religious paintings is shown wearing a blue cloak.

Self-confidence

Try this!

Be kind to yourself when you look in the mirror. Smile at your reflection and greet yourself in a friendly way, the way you would with other people you like. "Good to see you!" Or "Wow, you look great today!" Look at yourself calmly and identify what makes you the fantastic individual you are. Even if it feels weird, it will put you in a better mood.

When you are good at something, or try something new, you feel strong and sure inside. You gain confidence when you bake a cake by yourself for the first time, or after you finally overcome your reluctance to jump off the diving board at the pool. The more often you experience such moments, the more courageous you become over time.

Self-confidence means finding out what you can do and finding out what your own talents are. It also means knowing what you don't like so much. It doesn't matter what others do, how they behave or what they think of you. So, for example, it can also be just as confidence-building to decide to simply climb down from that diving board.

45

Self-doubt

Try this!

Decide on a day when you will act a bit differently from usual—maybe even a bit strangely. Perhaps this means wearing your little sister's pink glitter barrette in your hair or wearing two different shoes to school. Maybe you'll try out a new style of walking or dare to speak to someone you don't know.

Most people have moments when they don't feel like they're beautiful or cool enough. Often they secretly worry that people won't like them as much because of this. When you feel like this, it can help to think about what you like best about your own friends. Most of the time it has nothing to do with their beautiful complexion but is rather that you can do fun things together. It's not because of their body, but because it's great to talk and laugh together, maybe even argue. Friends are friends because they get along with each other. When it comes to friendship, how you look is pretty much irrelevant.

Not normal

If you watch videos on the internet or follow your friends on social media, you may sometimes feel you're different from everyone else. As if you're the only one who isn't happy with your appearance, who feels unsure, who isn't athletic, who doesn't have a dozen best friends, the only one who can't do something, the only one with an annoying family. You might be thinking, I'm the only one who isn't normal! At such moments you can feel sad and alone.

Your friends know what it's like to compare yourself to others. They've felt the same way. So it can be good to talk about it with each other. You'll quickly realize that it's pretty normal to not feel normal.

Embarrassment

When you're embarrassed, you suddenly no longer feel comfortable in your own skin. You may begin to sweat, your heart might beat faster or you might get red in the face. You want nothing more than to sink right into the ground. Even worse is when others make fun of you for it. Some people get embarrassed when they have to present in front of the class, others when they have to get changed at the swimming pool. Everyone in the world knows how awkward it feels to accidentally fart in public. Often it helps to have friends around to help you feel secure again more quickly.

But there's a useful side to shame, too. It reminds us to look after ourselves and can sometimes help us avoid getting in dangerous situations.

The way my face goes red when I'm embarrassed is incredibly embarrassing.

Family reunion 2014

Frida Rabia Louis Tina John

Helena

Turn to pages 28 and 34 to see how we used to look.

And to page 68 to see how we look later on.

Changes

From the moment you are born, your body keeps changing. No one can know how a newborn baby will look as an adult. Our bodies are constantly growing and changing. There is no break.

What will my body look like later on?

TOM   TINA

TRANS CHILDREN

LIV

CARL

50

Your body's changes are barely noticeable when you look at yourself in the mirror every day, but you can see them in photos taken from year to year. Your personality, too, grows and develops as you age.

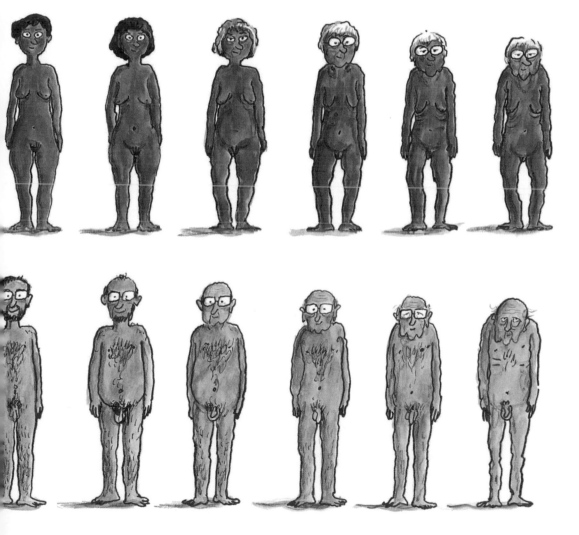

Puberty

Some of the biggest changes our bodies undergo are at puberty, which can be an exciting and tumultuous time. Within a few years, the body changes from that of a child to a teenager. Body parts grow and new hair sprouts. The shape of the body changes; it smells different and produces new liquids—discharge, menstrual blood or semen. It takes time to get used to all these new things.

It's not just the body that changes. Some teenagers become brave and self-confident. Others turn rather shy, while still others discover new talents—perhaps they're good at rapping, drawing or dancing.

People reach puberty at different times. Some feel the physical changes when they're eight or nine. Others might be fourteen and still waiting for puberty to start.

Desire

Sexual desire in puberty is a new sensation that you can feel all over your body. Your heart will beat faster, your nipples become firmer, your skin may feel all shivery. A soft, warm, swelling feeling can arise in the vagina or penis. Desire is such a wonderful tingly feeling that you want to experience it again and again.

Changing feelings

At some point it starts. Situations that were perfectly normal are suddenly uncomfortable. You may feel awkward talking to people, or maybe you no longer feel comfortable changing clothes in front of your own family.

Even your parents are suddenly embarrassing. They wear ridiculous clothes, ask your friends weird questions, bring your forgotten lunch into the classroom or shout at you from across the street. Usually it's not that your parents are acting particularly strangely, but that you are becoming more independent. More and more you want to form your own opinions and show the outside world that parents are no longer that important. This awkward feeling is part of growing up.

Being in love

You can be in love at any age, but for many it happens for the first time at puberty. It is particularly wonderful when two people feel the same way about each other. In moments of closeness, your bodies feel so intertwined that sometimes you completely forget what is happening around you, and it's hard to know who's who. Being in love makes you feel all warm inside, no matter how cold it is out. It's so exciting that your whole body feels tingly and bubbly, and you may hear your heart beating loudly.

Being in love can also hurt, and your body may feel a stab every time you think about the person you love. The combination of longing and love can result in a special intense sensation that makes you feel strong and weak at the same time.

Getting old

As people get older, you can see that their bodies age too. With time the body gets smaller and rounder or thinner, more wrinkled, more wobbly and a little weaker. Old people have known their bodies for a long time. They know where it sometimes hurts and what it needs. Just like young people, old people may feel lively and attractive on certain days. On other days they might prefer not to look in the mirror so much. Some people fall in love with their bodies all over again, change up their appearance or learn a new skill.

Ah, Josephine! That dress looks absolutely fabulous on you!

All kinds of hair

HAIRSTYLES

Some people are always changing their hairstyle. Others stick with the same haircut for many years. A new hairstyle can transform a person's appearance. Sometimes it takes a bit of courage to decide to switch to a new hairdo. Some people use wigs or extensions made from real or artificial hair as part of their hairstyles.

Some hairstyles

Some headgear

BODY HAIRSTYLES

Hairstyles can be found not just on the head, but wherever there is enough hair. Faces can have full beards, mustaches, sideburns, stubble, braided beards or goatees. People of all genders have facial hair—sometimes more, sometimes less, sometimes dark, sometimes light. Eyebrow, armpit, chest, leg and pubic hair can also be styled, trimmed, shaved, dyed, gelled and combed, depending on fashion and mood.

HAIR REMOVAL

Different people and cultures have different ideas about our hairy bodies and changing body hair. Sometimes this is for fun and sometimes it's a way to pressure people to conform—like the way many cultures expect women to remove their body hair.

Some people just let the hair grow all over their body. Some remove hair that grows in certain places. Some try leaving hair on some parts of their body and sometimes going without. Others remove every visible hair because they like their body completely smooth. Backs, legs, armpits, pubic hair and eyebrows are some of the many hairy places that people experiment with changing.

There are different ways to remove body hair. You can shave or pluck, or use wax, sugar paste or special creams. Everyone does it differently.

Body decoration

People all over the world have always decorated and altered their bodies. Some do it to show that they are especially brave; others to show that they belong to a particular group; still others do it just because they think it looks good. In different cultures a painful modification of the body can also be a ritual initiating a young person into the adult world.

With **tattooing**, pigment is placed under the skin with the help of needles or blades to create designs and drawings. Tattooing lines and patterns on the skin is an art that has been around for centuries. Traditional designs might show a person's tribal affiliation and position in society, describe their abilities and much more. Polynesian culture has a strong history of tattoo art, and our word derives from the Samoan word *tatau*.

Try this!

Body decoration often has a very personal meaning. The next time you get the chance, take a closer look at a person's body art and consider what kind of story might lie behind it.

Piercings are rings or rods that are attached to the body through holes in the skin. The most well-known piercings for us are earrings, but the ears, tongue, nose, nipples, penis and labia are just some of the other places where piercings are common. A piercing adorns and decorates a specific part of the body, sometimes making it more sensitive.

Body scarring is another kind of body decoration. A pattern is scratched or burned into the skin, and the healing of the skin is repeatedly disturbed so that deep scarring occurs. Among some African peoples elaborate scar patterns show someone's clan and whether the person is married.

Some body decorations leave marks that are very difficult to undo. Some remain forever.

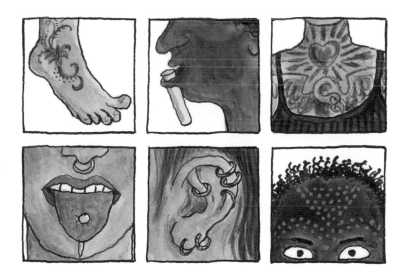

Body idioms

Do you know these idioms that use body parts to describe other things? See answers on page 90.

Makeup

Makeup isn't just for Halloween or costume parties. Both boys and girls try on makeup for fun, to see how different they can look to others. Some people wear makeup every day; others only for special occasions, while still others prefer to wear none at all. As long as people have existed, they have worn makeup. People have painted themselves during warfare, as camouflage, to slip into other roles in films or plays, or after accidents to cover up scars. Sometimes makeup is used on corpses to make them look more lifelike when they are lying in the coffin.

Cosmetic surgery

Some people are so unhappy with certain parts of their body that they decide to have an operation to change them—they might be unhappy about protruding ears or a very large nose, they might think their skin is too saggy or their breasts are too small. People undertake cosmetic surgery to repair damage from accidents or burns, or to change things that seriously affect their health, such as getting breast-reduction surgery.

Any cosmetic surgery is a serious procedure. Operations involve a degree of pain and bleeding, and can produce lasting scars. Specialist doctors help people decide whether surgery will help in their particular situation.

Beauty then & now

high forehead

HAIRLINE
PLUCKING

EYE LIFT

fox eyes

SKIN PIERCING

HAIR TRANSPLANT

lip plugs

tunnel
gauges

piercing

from belly
to head

TIGHTLY LACED
CORSET

HEAVY AND
BULKY WIGS

about to
faint

TEETH

black

gold

filed

BABY'S HEAD TIGHTLY WRAPPED

as tall and long as possible

Beauty yesterday, today & tomorrow

People have always done things to their bodies—to feel more beautiful, to show that they belong, or to be different from others.

Ancient Romans bleached their hair with pee because being blond was considered especially beautiful. In the sixteenth century it was considered stylish to have a high forehead, so many women plucked and shaved their forehead and eyebrows.

In the Baroque era, it was fashionable to be fat. Double chins were considered incredibly attractive. People sometimes wore extra padding under their clothes to make themselves look bigger. At other times, women gave themselves so-called wasp waists by squeezing themselves into stiff corsets. They would keep fainting because they couldn't breathe in enough air.

All over the world today, people still alter their bodies in ways they think are attractive or for cultural reasons.

What will it be like in the future? Maybe full body hair will be the new trend, as protection against strong sunlight. Maybe people will be able to exchange body parts. Perhaps everyone will want to look the same, wearing the same clothes and shoes.

Family reunion 2023

Turn to pages 28, 34 and 48 to see how we used to look.

68

First impressions

Try this!

The next time you meet someone new, write down your first impression. What kind of person are they? What do you like about them? After you've known the person for a while, you can look back to see what turned out to be true and where you were wrong.

Whenever you meet a new person, the first thing you take in is their body. How the person dresses, what kind of hairstyle they have, their gestures and voice. Even a person's distinctive smell will reach your nose, though you may not be aware of it. You'll form a first impression within a few seconds, and you might guess fairly quickly whether you like the other person or not.

What you experience in those first moments is just a tiny part of the other person, who is much more than how they look on the outside and still has a few surprises in store.

Needs to sleep with his teddy bear.

Has a black belt in karate.

70

Compliments

Try this!

When you're sitting with your friends or family, go around the group and ask everyone to give genuine compliments to one person at a time: "I like you because..." "It's good to do... with you." "I think the most beautiful thing about you is..." This game feels really good!

It feels good to hear your family and friends say nice things about you and your body. All of us could use a daily dose because each compliment you receive from someone else is like a protective layer. The more you receive, the thicker this layer becomes and the stronger and more secure you feel beneath it. Mean words and your own self-doubts can't penetrate so deeply.

Sometimes you may not trust yourself to say something nice to a friend, even if you're thinking it. Maybe you're worried it might be embarrassing. Maybe you're even a bit jealous of the other person. Maybe you're worried the other person might think you've got a crush on them.

When you give a compliment, you can feel a special kind of joy yourself. It's like watching a friend unwrap a birthday gift that you've carefully chosen just for them.

Take a look at some people enjoying giving and receiving compliments!

These compliments are from our research survey.

Turn the page!

Body language

Try this!

Boost your self-confidence when meeting someone new: first pause to feel the ground firmly beneath your feet, then stand up straight and walk directly up to them, calmly looking them in the eye. If you find yourself feeling uncertain along the way, deliberately say to yourself, "Here I come!"

When people meet each other, they communicate before they even say a word. Their bodies speak body language.

All over the world people's gestures and movements will express feelings like fear, joy, sadness or disgust. A smile can mean friendliness; pulling the eyebrows together can indicate growing anger; outstretched arms can mean welcome; a shy glance at the floor can show uncertainty.

Your facial expressions, gestures and posture tell people around you quite a lot about how you are doing.

Not everyone around the world understands gestures in the same way. A friendly or neutral gesture in one culture can mean something rude or threatening in another. In some cultures, nodding your head means Yes. In other cultures, it means No. The same is true for shaking your head side to side—it can mean opposite things in different places! It's a good idea to learn about gestures and body languages before you travel to a new place so you aren't sending the wrong message.

I'm open-minded.

I feel uncertain.

I'm feeling a bit shy right now.

I feel comfortable.

I feel irritated.

Please listen to me!

I'm feeling under pressure.

Here I am.

I'm paying attention to you.

I'm interested.

I'm not sure.

I'm not sure.

Touch

Most people feel good about being touched in a caring way by people they know—with a gentle hand on the back, a pat or a comforting hug. People who receive and give touch a lot tend to be particularly happy.

Try this!
With a friend, stretch out your index fingers and touch the tips together like the point of a roof. With the thumb and forefinger of your other hand, stroke the touching fingers at the same time. Who is feeling what?

Even when it is still in its mother's womb, a baby reaches for its own face and body. Maybe it's getting a sense of itself for the first time: "I am here." Later it learns from being cuddled and touched where its body begins and ends.

Babies who are born prematurely are placed on a parent's bare chest as often as possible. They feel secure and cozy there, and they'll gain weight twice as quickly with more touch.

Touch can also tickle, especially in the armpits, on the soles of the feet and on the belly. Feeling ticklish is actually your body's protective reaction, because you are particularly vulnerable in those spots. You can't tickle yourself, though, because your brain already knows that there is no real danger.

Touch is very personal. That's why each person needs to pay attention to what they and other people are comfortable with. What one person enjoys, another person might not, and this can change from day to day as well, or even in the moment. Everyone is allowed to change their mind about being touched.

Peer pressure

COMMENTING ON HOW OTHERS LOOK

Making comments about other people's bodies can be hurtful. Even when someone makes a comment in fun and doesn't mean to cause harm, it's often not funny at all for the person on the receiving end. They may pretend they don't care, even if it hurts inside. But people remember the mean things others have said and how painful it feels, sometimes for years!

Did you know?
For thousands of years our ancestors had to have good memories to remember which plants might be poisonous or which situations might be dangerous. So even today, people are still very good at remembering things that are mean or nasty.

CHALLENGES

A challenge can be a pretty outrageous task where one person tries to imitate or outdo another. Sometimes the challenge is filmed and shared on social media. You can find all sorts of new challenges on the internet. Some are just for fun. Others are for a good cause. But challenges can also become dangerous if they are based on dares, or if it's all about becoming better or thinner or braver than other people. Only take part in challenges if you really want to and not because you feel pressured to.

PHOTOS AND VIDEOS

Using filters and other effects on photos of yourself and your friends can be fun. Everything looks shinier and smoother than it is in real life. Almost all the pictures and videos that you see in ads and on the internet do this, too—they have been digitally enhanced so that what you see no longer looks like it did in real life.

Most people know this. Still, our brains take in the images as if they were real. So, for instance, we get the idea that it would be normal to have a body with no pimples, bumps or scars, or a body that is very slim. The more we see these images, the more we believe they are real. It's easy to forget that people change images to reflect their own culture, prejudices and biases.

79

NO!

It feels good to be close to people you know and trust. It can make you feel protected and secure to lie around on the sofa or read aloud together, cuddle up or be comforted. But being close may not always feel that way.

Sometimes touching or even words can suddenly feel too close. Even if the other person is someone you know, you can get a strange and uncomfortable feeling that doesn't feel good. Sometimes touch or words can be downright unpleasant, making you want to get away from the situation. Maybe you want to fight back, but you don't dare. Sometimes touching can hurt or even injure. That is violence, and violence is not okay.

As soon as you feel weird or uncomfortable, as soon as someone comes too close, it is important and completely acceptable to say NO out loud. Even to adults.

Try this!

Be the boss of your own back massage. Lie on your belly and tell the other person how you want to be massaged—kneaded, tapped or rubbed. The other person must do everything you say: "A little harder, please… just a bit farther up… yes, right there…" When you have had enough, switch roles.

Everyone has the right to say no. It's a good idea to seek support from a friend, your parents or an adult you trust. Each person has their own feelings about how close they want to get to others. It is different for everyone, and those feelings can change from day to day. Everyone should decide for themselves who is allowed to be close to them and in what way. And others must respect this choice.

Choosing for yourself

Your body belongs to you.

Sometimes parents will want to make decisions about their child's body. They may forget that it is just as important for a child to learn to consider what's best for them and their own body. Even if it may be frustrating for adults, every child has the right to have control over their own body.

81

At home

For each of us, our body acts as a home. So it's good if we can enjoy living in it. None of us can decide ahead of time who our parents will be or which country we'll be born in. In the same way, we can't choose which physical characteristics we will come into the world with. But one thing we can all do is figure out how to feel at home in our own body.

AND NOW YOU!

YES NO

☐ ☐ I'm ticklish.

☐ ☐ I think every day about the way I look.

☐ ☐ I know what my feet smell like at the end of the day.

☐ ☐ I look at myself naked in the mirror.

☐ ☐ I'm envious when I see other people looking beautiful.

☐ ☐ I exercise to feel good in my body.

☐ ☐ I like my head being scratched.

☐ ☐ I've been told that I'm beautiful.

☐ ☐ There are at least three parts of my body I'd like to change.

☐ ☐ There is one part of my body that looks exactly like the same part on a relative.

☐ ☐ My farts smell good.

☐ ☐ Sometimes I pull faces in the mirror..

☐ ☐ I know a place where my skin is especially soft.

☐ ☐ If I were granted one wish for my body, I know what I would wish for!

☐ ☐ I can't walk past a mirror without looking at my reflection.

☐ ☐ I have swum naked.

☐ ☐ I think I have nice-looking feet.

☐ ☐ I know what shape my father's eyes are.

☐ ☐ I have eaten my own boogers.

☐ ☐ I often think about the way other people look.

☐ ☐ I have an outie belly button.

☐ ☐ I can do a trick with my body that most people can't.

☐ ☐ I've seen family members naked.

☐ ☐ I think armpit hair looks nice.

☐ ☐ I wish I knew what my body will look like in ten years.

☐ ☐ Someone once said something mean about my body.

☐ ☐ I know what pee smells like.

☐ ☐ I think tattoos are beautiful.

☐ ☐ I'd like to be a different gender for one day.

☐ ☐ I have won an arm-wrestling contest.

☐ ☐ I know whether my earlobes are attached or not.

☐ ☐ Sometimes I wonder how others see me.

☐ ☐ I have one mole I like best.

☐ ☐ I once said something mean about someone else's body.

☐ ☐ I like to take selfies.

☐ ☐ If I had another body, I would be a completely different person.

☐ ☐ I have a scar that reminds me of an old injury.

☐ ☐ I know what it's like to feel different.

☐ ☐ I talk to myself in the mirror.

☐ ☐ My body is fine the way it is.

☐ ☐ I'm more like my mother than my father.

☐ ☐ Sometimes I just think I'm so _____.

THIS IS ME

Draw yourself and highlight these places.

I like these parts the best.

I'm especially ticklish right here.

I obviously inherited this body part from _ _ _ _ _ _ .

I am particularly strong here.

This spot is a bit unusual.

Index of headings

Answers to the body idioms on page 62

Put a bug in your ear.
A head-turner.
Light a fire under your butt.
She's wrapped around your finger.
Your heart in your mouth.
A frog in your throat.

This edition first published in 2023 by Gecko Press
PO Box 9335, Wellington 6141, Aotearoa New Zealand
office@geckopress.com

English-language edition © Gecko Press Ltd 2023
Translation © Shelley Tanaka 2023

Original title: *Any Body: Dick & dünn & Haut & Haar: das große Abc von unserem Körper-Zuhause* © 2021 Klett Kinderbuch, Leipzig, Germany

Gecko Press is committed to sustainable practice. We publish books to be read over and over. We use sewn bindings and high-quality production, and print all our new books using vegetable-based inks on FSC-certified paper from sustainably managed forests.

The translation of this work was supported by a grant from the Goethe-Institut

GOETHE
INSTITUT

Original language: German
Cover design by Vida Kelly
Printed in China by Everbest Printing Co. Ltd,
an accredited ISO 14001 & FSC-certified printer

ISBN: 9781776575466

For more curiously good books, visit geckopress.com

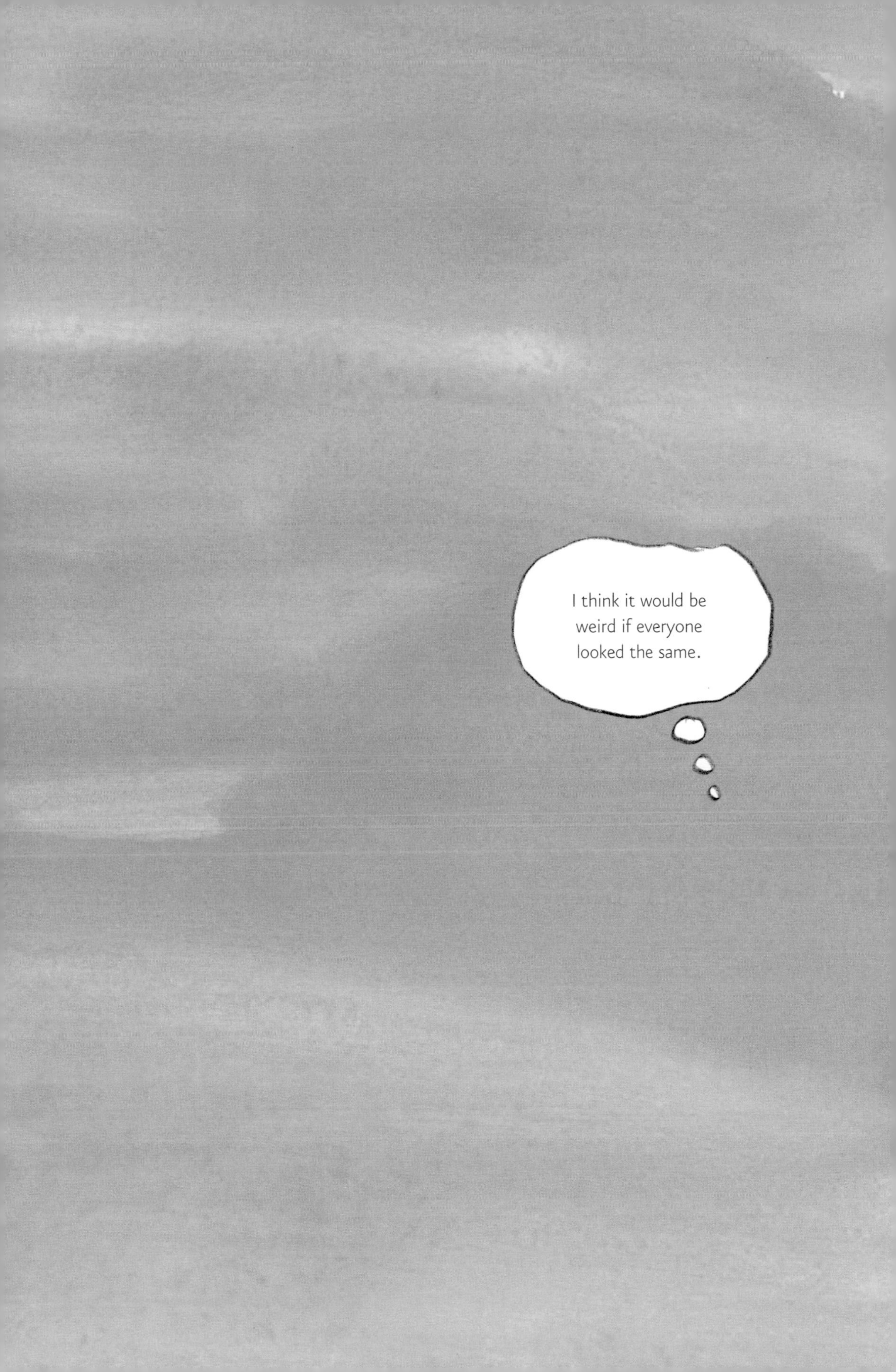
I think it would be weird if everyone looked the same.

I am quite tall. When I go to the movies, I get cramps in my calves if there isn't enough room for my legs.

I have a lot of tattoos. My tattoos help me to love my body.

I wish I had smaller feet so I could fit into my rubber boots again.

My hair is nice and long and thick. I have enough to make myself a little beard if I ever need one, and I don't even need to wear a scarf in the winter!

Maybe I'll have breast surgery one day.

I like my hands. They're big compared to the rest of my body, and they are extremely strong from pushing my wheelchair around all day.

I have many parts that aren't perfect, but they all belong to me and make me who I am. Without them, I wouldn't be me.

I have a big butt. I like to call it "my pillow."

Sometimes I think my body is a little too thin. It bothers me when other people can see my ribs. Then I think, well, that's just the way it is and I've always been like this. It's all good.

I say sorry to my body when I wear uncomfortable clothes or when I've been working too much.

Sometimes I wish I looked different. I'd like to have a beard or a penis and no boobs.

Sometimes I catch myself thinking I'm lucky because I'm not as fat as that woman over there. I think that's mean of me.

What if our faces were upside down, with eyes at the bottom and mouth on top? Or if our feet pointed backwards?